HOUSTON ASTROS

IQ

THE ULTIMATE TEST OF TRUE FANDOM

Copyright © 2019 Tucker Elliot.

All rights reserved.

ISBN: 978-0-9912699-7-6

Special thanks to Dan "One Win" Monfre.

Front cover photo courtesy of Chiti Ho.

Interior layout and formatting by BMP Digital.

Black Mesa

Florida

CONTENTS

	INTRODUCTION	i
1	THE NUMBERS GAME	1
2	BASEBALL QUOTES	15
3	WORLD SERIES CHAMPIONS	27
4	FRANCHISE LEADERS	41
5	OCTOBER BASEBALL	51
6	FANTASTIC FEATS	63
7	AWARD WINNERS	75
8	THE TEAMS	85
9	ANALYTICS	97
10	EXTRA INNINGS	109

INTRODUCTION

Arthur Daley, the Pulitzer Prize-winning sportswriter for the *New York Times*, wrote more than eleven thousand daily columns and twenty million words covering sports all over the world—but his favorite sport was baseball, and on that subject he famously wrote, "A baseball fan has the digestive apparatus of a billy goat. He can, and does, devour any set of statistics with insatiable appetite and then nuzzles hungrily for more."

Daley was right, of course.

Baseball relies on numbers and statistics more than any other sport—and we use those numbers to measure success and failure, they guide our decisions in playing and managing the game, they fuel our discussions when watching the game as a spectator or reliving it over the water cooler at work, and they keep us awake late at night, celebrating or lamenting, depending on, well, the final score.

Numbers, for the most part, don't lie.

Statistics on the other hand ... well, it depends who you ask.

Bob Woolf was a Boston lawyer and a pioneer in the business of representing athletes in contract negotiations and sponsorship deals. In other words, he was one of the first sports agents. Woolf related this anecdote about Boston Red Sox pitcher Bob Stanley: "When I negotiated his contract with the Red Sox, we had statistics demonstrating he was the third best pitcher in the league. They had a chart showing he was the sixtieth best pitcher in the Red Sox organization." Perhaps it's the ability to manipulate and interpret statistics that makes numbers so fascinating to baseball fans.

Here's what I know about baseball and numbers that is incontrovertible: Math was my favorite grade school subject because it was the easiest. I knew it already from calculating batting averages and earned run averages and projecting how many hits and RBIs I'd have at the end of the season based on the games I'd already played—math skills that were easily three or four years ahead of my grade level at the time. My mom was the official scorekeeper at our Little League games and we'd spend hours each week pouring through the scorebook, tabulating all the stats, and then placing them in columns and charts on construction paper as if it was the back of my very own Topps baseball card.

Numbers resonate with baseball fans, no question about it.

It's not just the stats, either. We use numbers to track the performance of our favorite players, sure, but we also use numbers to identify them—as in jersey numbers. I met Johnny Bench once during spring training. Big surprise—I wore #5 a few weeks later when my summer league kicked off. You can track my idols using my Little League and high school jersey numbers: #5 (Bench), #8 (Gary Carter), #23 (Don Mattingly), and #8 again (Cal Ripken Jr.). There's a very good reason why franchises retire jersey numbers to honor their most important stars—just as a fan wearing a #27 Astros jersey is making a statement about Jose Altuve's contributions to the club, when the club retires a number it's making a statement about that player's significance to the history of the entire organization.

This is a book of trivia, but it is derived from numbers.

And collectively they tell the story of the Houston Astros.

Now step up to the plate.

Challenge yourself.

Enjoy, and reminisce.

This is your Houston Astros IQ, the ultimate test of true fandom.

"To the Astros fans … you guys are the greatest fans in the world."

— *Craig Biggio*

1 THE NUMBERS GAME

Any self-respecting fan should be able to cite the most notable and historic stats in franchise history—and you should also be able to identify the most revered jersey numbers as well. Astros history is replete with superstars and individuals who distinguished themselves as fan-favorites, and that's why we open the top of the first with a simple numbers game: Do you know the jersey numbers for these all-time greats?

TOP OF THE FIRST

Q1: Jeff Bagwell made 15 consecutive Opening Day starts at first base for the Astros from 1991-2005. He's a baseball legend, and as such was enshrined at Cooperstown in 2017. What jersey number did the Astros retire in honor of Bagwell in 2007?
- a) 3
- b) 5
- c) 8
- d) 11

Q2: Craig Biggio made 19 consecutive Opening Day starts for the Astros during 20 big league seasons. He was the first player in franchise history to join the exclusive 3,000-hit club. Biggio was enshrined at Cooperstown in 2015. What jersey number did the Astros retire in honor of Biggio in 2008?
- a) 4
- b) 7
- c) 14
- d) 17

Q3: Jimmy Wynn—affectionately referred to as the "Toy Cannon"—played 11 seasons in Houston and hit 223 home runs. He was one of Houston's first superstars and still ranks among the top 10 in numerous offensive categories. What jersey number did the Astros retire in honor of Wynn in 2005?
- a) 4
- b) 14
- c) 24
- d) 34

Q4: Jose Cruz was the Astros' team MVP four times and he was the first player in franchise history to hit over .300 in six different seasons. He would later return to the club as a coach. What jersey number did the Astros retire in honor of Cruz in 1992?

   a) 5
   b) 15
   c) 25
   d) 35

Q5: Jim Umbricht was an original member of the Houston Colt .45s. He was selected from Pittsburgh during the expansion draft in 1961—and in 1962, he appeared in 34 games and was 4-0 with a 2.01 ERA. Umbricht was diagnosed with cancer in March 1963, but less than two months removed from surgery he was back on the mound and was one of the league's top relief pitchers for the remainder of the season. Tragically, Umbricht died of lymphoma in 1964. His number was the first in franchise history to be retired—and in 2019, he was an inaugural member of the Houston Astros Hall of Fame. What jersey number did the Astros retire in honor of Umbricht in 1965?

   a) 12
   b) 22
   c) 32
   d) 42

Q6: Mike Scott played nine seasons with the Astros and for a five-year stretch from 1985-89 he was one of the most dominant pitchers in the game. What jersey number did the Astros retire in honor of Scott in 1992?

   a) 33
   b) 34

c) 35
d) 36

Q7: Jackie Robinson broke baseball's color barrier in 1947. Fifty years later every MLB franchise retired his #42 jersey to commemorate Robinson's courageous legacy. Robinson is the only player to ever be honored in such a way. However, there are several players who have retired numbers with two different teams—and two players have seen their jersey numbers retired by *three* MLB clubs: Frank Robinson (Reds, Orioles, Indians) and Nolan Ryan (Angels, Astros, Rangers). Ryan is baseball's all-time leader in strikeouts—and 1,866 came during the nine seasons he spent in Houston. What jersey number did the Astros retire in honor of Ryan in 1996?
  a) 30
  b) 34
  c) 40
  d) 44

Q8: Don Wilson made his big league debut with one start in 1966. He was a mainstay in the rotation for eight seasons from 1967-74, and won more than 100 games for the Astros. Wilson and his five-year-old son died in a tragic accident in January 1975. In April, on the final day of the season's first homestand, the Astros retired his jersey number. What jersey number did the Astros retire in honor of Wilson?
  a) 20
  b) 30
  c) 40
  d) 60

Q9: Larry Dierker was an 18-year-old kid when he made his big league debut for the Colt .45s in September 1964. All he did was strike out Willie Mays in the first inning. Dierker won 137 games in 13 seasons with the club—and later would spend 18 seasons as a team broadcaster and another five as manager. What jersey number did the Astros retire in honor of Dierker in 2002?

    a) 43
    b) 45
    c) 47
    d) 49

Q10: Roger Clemens only pitched three seasons for the Astros, but in that time he won a Cy Young Award and was instrumental in the club making its first-ever appearance in the World Series. What jersey number did Clemens wear during his tenure with the Astros?

    a) 11
    b) 12
    c) 21
    d) 22

TOP OF THE FIRST ANSWER KEY

1: b. 5.

2: b. 7.

3: c. 24.

4: c. 25.

5: c. 32.

6: a. 33.

7: b. 34.

8: c. 40.

9: d. 49.

10: d. 22.

BOTTOM OF THE FIRST

Q11: Roy Oswalt was 14-3 as a rookie and led the league with a .824 winning percentage in 2001. In any other season he would have been Rookie of the Year—but 2001 was the year of Albert Pujols. After a 19-win sophomore campaign that solidified his reputation as one of the top starters in the league, Oswalt shared with ESPN.com how he was influenced by Nolan Ryan: "I grew up watching Nolan Ryan. I liked the way he pitched. He pitched aggressive—went right after guys, knocked down guys when he needed to. Just to be able to throw the ball by guys is a rush. Especially when a guy is sitting on a fastball and you actually throw it by him to defeat him. That's a lot better than tricking him." Oswalt would go on to win 129 games from 2001-08, the highest total in the NL for that period. The only pitcher close to that total was Greg Maddux with 115 wins. What jersey number did Oswalt wear during his tenure with the Astros?

   a) 43
   b) 44
   c) 45
   d) 46

Q12: Lance Berkman played 12 seasons in Houston and was one of the most prolific hitters in team history. He ranks at or near the top of dozens of offensive categories. Berkman had a stretch from 2001-08 in which he had 879 RBIs. That total was the second highest in the NL in that time—only Albert Pujols had more. In 2005, Berkman hit a playoff grand slam vs. the Braves that will be remembered as one of the most clutch hits in franchise history—and when that club won the pennant, he said: "It's unbelievable, I can't even describe it. To be part of bringing the first World Series to

Houston is just tremendous." What was Berkman's primary jersey number during his tenure with the Astros?

    a) 12
    b) 17
    c) 22
    d) 27

Q13: In 1993, Houston traded Eric Anthony to the Seattle Mariners in exchange for Mike Felder and Mike Hampton—and that acquisition proved to be a big reason the Astros won three consecutive division titles from 1997-99. Mike Hampton had a four-year stretch from 1996-99 in which he was one of the game's most dominant lefties and won 58 games—including a league best 22 in 1999. Hampton would wear three different jersey numbers during two stints with the Astros. What was his primary number with the club?

    a) 10
    b) 11
    c) 32
    d) 38

Q14: Billy Wagner was one of the game's dominant closers during nine seasons in Houston—and he saved a franchise record 225 games. Randy Johnson, who was with the Astros for a short time in 1998, had this to say about his teammate: "The first time I met him, I thought, 'He's a foot shorter than me, and throws harder than I do.'" Wagner could flat bring the heater—and while he never led the NL in saves, he did establish a franchise record with 44 saves in 2003 and he owns four of the top 10 season totals in Astros history. What jersey number did Wagner wear during his tenure with the Astros?

    a) 1

b) 3
c) 13
d) 31

Q15: In an article for MLB.com, Alyson Footer refers to Bill Doran as a "scrappy second baseman who was an ingredient of some of the most exciting squads in franchise history"—including the 1986 club that lost a heart-breaking NLCS to the New York Mets. Doran played nine seasons for Houston and ranks second in franchise history for hits by a switch-hitter. Only Lance Berkman had more. What jersey number did Doran wear during his tenure with the Astros?

    a) 13
    b) 19
    c) 23
    d) 29

Q16: Kevin Bass gave an interview once, in which he admitted: "I really loved playing football. I had aspirations to play college football. My junior year of high school, I decided to just skip basketball and focus on lifting to get strong for my senior year of football. When baseball started, scouts started coming out to watch me play. After being drafted, I was flattered and surprised." Bass came to Houston to complete a trade that sent Hall of Famer Don Sutton to Milwaukee—and he contributed his finest offensive season to the 1986 division champion Astros. He was an All-Star that season, and batted .311 with a career best 20 home runs. He ranks third in franchise history for home runs by a switch-hitter—but he's the only Astros player to hit a home run from both sides of the plate in the same game … *three* times. Bass wore several different jersey numbers in his career. What was his primary number with the Astros?

a) 8
b) 17
c) 20
d) 21

Q17: Bob Watson spent 14 seasons with Houston and was a two-time All-Star. Watson's 1,381 games still rank among the top 10 totals in franchise history. He has the distinction of being the first player in franchise history with 100 RBIs in a season in which he hit fewer than 20 home runs. In 1976, he hit 16 home runs with 102 RBIs. That season he was also top 10 in the league with 183 hits and 268 total bases. Watson's baseball career continued long after his playing days were over. He would go on to serve as general manager of the Yankees and Astros and as a vice president of Major League Baseball. Watson wore four different numbers as he was up and down from the minors early in his Astros career … but what was his primary jersey number from 1968-79?
a) 11
b) 26
c) 27
d) 38

Q18: Joe Morgan was up for a few games in 1963 and 1964, and at the end of his career he did a second tour of duty in Houston for one season in 1980—but it was seven seasons from 1965-71 that set the second baseman's career on a Hall of Fame trajectory. Morgan was second in Rookie of the Year balloting in 1965. He led the league in walks with 97 and led the team with 100 runs scored, and for the rest of his career he was notorious for working the count and getting free passes. In parts of 10 seasons with Houston he walked 678 times but had just 415 strikeouts. His career numbers were even better—he walked nearly twice as many times as he struck out. He wasn't playing today's game, that's for sure. Morgan wore four different numbers in his days with the Colt .45s and Astros. What was his jersey number from 1965-71?

    a) 8
    b) 12
    c) 18
    d) 35

Q19: The only team in the NL that hit fewer home runs than the Astros from 1985-90 was the St. Louis Cardinals. The Mets hit 945 home runs in that span—the highest total in the league—but the Astros hit just 655. And if not for Glenn Davis, the Astros' power outage would have been even worse. Davis hit 164 of Houston's 655 home runs in that six-year stretch—fully 25 percent of the team total. Only two NL sluggers amassed more home runs in that same period—Darryl Strawberry and Dale Murphy. Glenn Davis had more home runs than Ryne Sandberg, Howard Johnson, Kevin Mitchell, Mike Schmidt, Barry Bonds, Will Clark … all of them. Not bad, right? What jersey number did Davis wear during his tenure with the Astros?

    a) 7
    b) 17
    c) 27
    d) 37

Q20: Alan Ashby is second in franchise history with 868 games played at catcher. He hit 69 career home runs as a catcher—which doesn't sound like much, but it's the highest total in franchise history. He also played his home games at the Astrodome in the mid-1980s when Glenn Davis was practically the only guy who could go yard. Ashby was instrumental in three division titles during that time as well. What jersey number did Ashby wear during his tenure with the Astros?

    a) 8
    b) 10
    c) 12
    d) 14

BOTTOM OF THE FIRST ANSWER KEY

11: b. 44.

12: b. 17.

13: a. 10.

14: c. 13.

15: b. 19.

16: b. 17.

17: c. 27.

18: c. 18.

19: c. 27.

20: d. 14.

"I'm a professional ballplayer and what I see as my responsibility is to be ready to play. All the rest of that stuff, being a star or whatever, is never something I've been interested in."

— *Jeff Bagwell*

2 BASEBALL QUOTES

No other sport inspires quotes like baseball. Dozens of books are out there filled with nothing but quotes from the game's great players, managers, umpires, writers, and broadcasters. One reason we're fascinated with baseball quotes is because they tell us the history of the game in the words of those who were there to make or witness firsthand the plays that inspired generations of fans.

And lucky for us, baseball has inspired more written words than any other sport. Here in the second our trivia is inspired by our love for baseball quotes.

TOP OF THE SECOND

Q21: This player had some touching words for his father: "You used to say that you gave me your right arm throwing to me batting practice all the time, and you did. But more importantly, you taught me how to be a man, showed me respect, how to have respect, to walk through this life as a man."
    a) Lance Berkman
    b) Craig Biggio
    c) Jeff Bagwell
    d) Joe Morgan

Q22: This player hit one of the most important home runs in franchise history, but he would later recall: "I remember going up to bat, I was going to bunt. I remember literally walking up to bat and going, 'Man, Chipper Jones has been playing third base for six hours, no way is he ready to field a bunt right now."
    a) Brad Ausmus
    b) Chris Burke
    c) Orlando Palmeiro
    d) Lance Berkman

Q23: Hall of Fame legend Joe Morgan said of this player: "He had the greatest stuff I have ever seen and it still gives me goose bumps to think of what he might have become."
    a) Darryl Kile
    b) Brandon Backe
    c) J.R. Richard
    d) Jim Ray

Q24: This player shared a humorous baseball story with *Sports*

Illustrated: "In Baltimore last year I forgot how many outs there were and ran off the field. I got to the line, and nobody else is running off. I immediately went to the fake knee injury. The trainer came running out and was like, 'Are you OK?' And I said, 'Yeah, I just forgot how many outs there were.'"

    a) Lance Berkman
    b) Brad Ausmus
    c) Craig Biggio
    d) Jeff Bagwell

Q25: This player had some great advice for young players: "I've always believed in leading by doing it on the field … I've never thought that you have to be too outspoken in the clubhouse, as long as you set an example for guys to follow. People watch that more than they listen to some guy talking, no matter who he is."

    a) Hunter Pence
    b) Ty Wigginton
    c) Morgan Ensberg
    d) Roy Oswalt

Q26: Former Rangers' manager Ron Washington drily observed: "He's a pretty good hitter. That's why he leads the league."

    a) Jose Altuve
    b) Lance Berkman
    c) Craig Biggio
    d) Jeff Bagwell

Q27: This player had some advice for aspiring pitchers in *Baseball Digest*: "If you can get a guy to pull your best fastball, you've got him. He has no chance unless he has been guessing. If he normally hits that way, he can't hit any kind of breaking ball or off-speed pitch."

    a) Nolan Ryan

b) Joe Niekro
c) Larry Dierker
d) Mike Scott

Q28: This player emphasized the team aspect of baseball: "I was one of the guys that did all they could to win. I'm proud of my stats, but … if I stole a base, it was to help us win a game, and I like to think that's what made me special."
a) Craig Biggio
b) Joe Morgan
c) Cesar Cedeno
d) Bill Doran

Q29: The Astros lost 106, 107, and 111 games from 2011-13. That painful rebuild was a trying time for an organization—and more importantly, its fans—that has now won 101, 103, and 107 games from 2017-19. In 2014, general manager Jeff Luhnow indicated to ESPN that the club had finally turned the corner: "We don't want to rest all our hopes on one player, but [he's] a pretty good player and there's more behind him. If he does well, I think it will lift the city's spirits and give us hope that there's more like him coming."
a) Jose Altuve
b) George Springer
c) Marwin Gonzalez
d) Carlos Correa

Q30: This former player told the *Houston Chronicle*: "I don't know if I could make this team [2018 Astros]. The Yankees have tradition, the Dodgers have tradition, and the Astros have always just been this team down in Houston … [but] baseball is a game of hills and valleys and, right now, the Astros are on a hill and they're going to be good for a long time."

a) Jim Deshaies
b) Billy Wagner
c) Mike Scott
d) Brad Lidge

TOP OF THE SECOND ANSWER KEY

21: c. Jeff Bagwell.

22: b. Chris Burke.

23: c. J.R. Richard.

24: a. Lance Berkman.

25: d. Roy Oswalt.

26: a. Jose Altuve.

27: c. Larry Dierker.

28: b. Joe Morgan (Hall of Fame induction speech).

29: b. George Springer.

30: c. Mike Scott.

BOTTOM OF THE SECOND

Q31: This player was a heavily recruited running back in high school. He told the *Houston Chronicle*, "Truly, what I wanted to do was football. When it was taken away from me, being able to go to a big-time school, I just said: 'Get your act together.'"
　a) Lance Berkman
　b) Jeff Bagwell
　c) Ken Caminiti
　d) Craig Biggio

Q32: This player hit a ball completely out of Crosley Field in Cincinnati and onto the exit ramp of the highway that ran beside it. He would later comment: "I'm just swingin' the bat and lettin' wood meet horsehide."
　a) Ron Davis
　b) Rusty Staub
　c) Jimmy Wynn
　d) Joe Morgan

Q33: This pitcher famously said: "It helps if the hitter thinks you're a little crazy."
　a) Mike Hampton
　b) Nolan Ryan
　c) J.R. Richard
　d) Joe Niekro

Q34: Hall of Fame legend Joe Morgan said of this player: "One of the best and most underrated players I have ever seen."
　a) Jose Cruz
　b) Dan Driessen

c) Gerald Young
d) Cliff Johnson

Q35: This player was given credit for scoring the one millionth run in baseball history. The actual accounting of baseball's first million runs is still debated today. It's irrelevant to Astros fans. Some thirty-odd years later, this player would reflect: "I think my fan mail was something like four or five letters a week … scoring the one millionth run, it increased to fifty to one hundred per week. It got me on the map a little bit, and I ended up being the answer to a trivia question."
a) Cesar Cedeno
b) Bob Watson
c) Jose Cruz
d) Cliff Johnson

Q36: A positive assessment from Larry Dierker, whose association with the Astros dates to the earliest years in club history and includes time as both player and manager, carries significant weight. He had this to say as he spoke fondly of a former teammate: "He was, really, in many ways the ultimate ballplayer. He seemed to fit into the baseball life better than just about anyone I knew. Plus, he was pretty darn good at it."
a) Joe Niekro
b) Jose Cruz
c) Ken Forsch
d) Tommy Helms

Q37: Sportswriter Paul Ladewski wrote of this player: "[He] has averaged 27 home runs a season despite playing his home games inside the Astrodome and despite having no protection to speak of in the lineup. One can only wonder what the Georgia native would do if he were sandwiched between Ron Gant and Dave Justice in

Atlanta."
a) Kevin Bass
b) Ken Caminiti
c) Eric Anthony
d) Glenn Davis

Q38: Manager A.J. Hinch said of this pitcher: "He's the definition of an ace." And soon after, when the club faced another tough game, he reiterated: "He's our ace. He's our guy. So to hand him the ball with the season on the line—pretty awesome."
a) Dallas Keuchel
b) Justin Verlander
c) Gerrit Cole
d) Zack Greinke

Q39: This player fired up both fans and teammates with a walk-off home run in a crucial playoff game. He was just getting started in terms of "firing" things up. He took advantage of the inevitable TV cameras and microphones and lit a media firestorm with this bold statement: "In this jungle called the American League, we're the apex predator."
a) Alex Bregman
b) Carlos Correa
c) Jose Altuve
d) George Springer

Q40: This player busted out of a postseason slump with a grand slam that will undoubtedly live forever in Astros history … and afterward, he said, "I'd like to thank all the people on Twitter. They're my hitting coach. I got about 500 million tweets the last few days, so I appreciate that."
a) Alex Bregman

b) Carlos Correa
c) Jose Altuve
d) George Springer

BOTTOM OF THE SECOND ANSWER KEY

31: d. Craig Biggio.

32: c. Jimmy Wynn (1967).

33: b. Nolan Ryan.

34: a. Jose Cruz.

35: b. Bob Watson (1975).

36: a. Joe Niekro.

37: d. Glenn Davis.

38: a. Dallas Keuchel.

39: b. Carlos Correa (2019).

40: a. Alex Bregman (2019).

"We're coming home a champion, Houston."
— *George Springer*

3 WORLD SERIES CHAMPIONS

The story of baseball in Houston begins in 1962 at the mosquito-infested Colt Stadium. It's pinnacle came in 2017, when the Astros defeated the Los Angeles Dodgers to win the World Series.

It took 56 years.

Most were frustrating. Some were oh-so-gloriously close. Ten times in 55 seasons the Astros made the playoffs. Only once in ten Octobers did the club claim a pennant.

The most difficult year had to be 2013.

The club switched leagues, and lost 111 games. That's tough on players and fans, but when you consider the club had also lost 107 and 106 games in the two previous seasons, well … how exactly do you ask for resilience when the valley is so deep?

And yet.

Solid draft picks. Some key free agent signings. Hope in the form of a wild-card berth. Disappointment. Regression, more frustration.

Then, 2017.

At the trade deadline, the Astros got the final piece of the puzzle that the front office had been assembling for years: Justin Verlander.

101 regular season wins.

Take out the Red Sox in the LDS.

Take out the Yankees in the LCS.

Take out the Dodgers in the WS.

It took 56 years, but as they say: worth it.

Here in the third, the trivia is about the season-long journey of the 2017 World Series Champions.

TOP OF THE THIRD

Q41: Dallas Keuchel blanked the Mariners for seven innings in a 3-0 Opening Day victory to start 2017. He also blanked the Indians for seven innings in a 2-0 victory on Opening Day 2015—which made him the only pitcher in team history to achieve this feat twice. Who was the first pitcher in Astros history to pitch seven scoreless innings in an Opening Day victory?
 a) Shane Reynolds
 b) Mike Scott
 c) Nolan Ryan
 d) Roy Oswalt

Q42: Houston swept its opening series vs. Seattle when this player hit the Astros' only walk-off home run of 2017. It was plenty dramatic: Extra-innings, two outs, full count, Mariners ahead, 3-2. It made people believe this team was destined for something special—which, of course, it was. Whose walk-off home run inspired Astros fans and swept the Mariners?
 a) George Springer
 b) Jose Altuve
 c) Alex Bregman
 d) Brian McCann

Q43: The Astros won 23 of 34 games to start 2017, but a mid-May series in the Bronx is what made the rest of baseball take notice that this club was legit. The Yankees had won 21 of 31 to start the season, but the Astros took three out of four in that series—including the opener, which ended with the tying run being thrown out at the plate by an Astros outfielder. It was the first time an Astros outfielder threw out a runner at the plate to end a game since Darin Erstad in

2008—and the throw was so perfect, that the outfielder responsible for it began to celebrate even before catcher Brian McCann made the tag. Whose spectacular throw set the tone for this crucial series?
  a) George Springer
  b) Josh Reddick
  c) Norichika Aoki
  d) Jake Marisnick

Q44: Carlos Correa hit his 50th career home run in 2017. It took Correa just 298 games to reach that milestone—and in that span he had 321 total hits. Correa was just the second player in Astros history with 300 hits and 50 home runs in his first 300 career games. Who else achieved this feat?
  a) Jeff Bagwell
  b) Jose Altuve
  c) Glenn Davis
  d) Lance Berkman

Q45: In May 2017, both the AL Player of the Month and AL Pitcher of the month were on the Astros' roster. A.J. Hinch said: "We're playing well as a team. We've got some individual guys that got some awards, which is nice and well-deserved." For Player of the Month, this guy hit .386 with an 1.130 OPS, seven home runs, and 26 RBIs. Who posted these monster numbers?
  a) Jose Altuve
  b) Carlos Correa
  c) Alex Bregman
  d) George Springer

Q46: And a follow-up … for Pitcher of the Month, this guy went 4-0 with a 0.99 ERA in six starts. He gave up just four earned runs in 36 1/3 innings—and he struck out 37 batters. Who was the best

pitcher in the AL during May 2017?
   a) Lance McCullers
   b) Dallas Keuchel
   c) Mike Fiers
   d) Brad Peacock

Q47: The 2017 Astros had 60 wins at the All-Star break for the first time in franchise history. Heroics were a near-nightly occurrence. Same outcome, different player. Or in a game against the Twins … same outcome, *every* player. Minnesota led 8-2 in the top of the eighth—and Houston had never won a game when trailing by six or more runs in the eighth inning or later: 0-921 all-time. Houston sent 15 batters to the plate and scored 11 runs en route to a 16-8 victory. Who put an exclamation mark on that historic eighth-inning rally with a three-run home run?
   a) Brian McCann
   b) Carlos Beltran
   c) Evan Gattis
   d) Josh Reddick

Q48: Justin Verlander led the league with 23 quality starts in 2017. Only five of his 33 starts came after he was traded to Houston at the end of August. How many quality starts did Verlander make for the Astros in September 2017?
   a) 0
   b) 1
   c) 3
   d) 5

Q49: By definition a "late and close" situation is "the seventh inning or later with the hitter's team tied, ahead by one, or has the tying run on base, at bat, or on deck" (MLB.com). In other words, clutch. This player was 19-for-41 in late and close situations for the Astros in 2017—including two home runs, eight RBIs, and 12 runs. He had an incredible .542 on-base percentage with the game on the line. Who posted these extraordinary numbers?

a) Carlos Beltran
b) Jose Altuve
c) Josh Reddick
d) Yuli Gurriel

Q50: In July 2017, this player hit safely in 19 consecutive games. It was the longest streak of the season for the Astros, but it wasn't even close to the most impressive number he posted that month. He batted .485 in 99 at-bats—a franchise record average for a full calendar month—and he had 48 hits, which was the highest monthly total since Lance Berkman had 49 in May 2008. The *Houston Chronicle* announced he had won the AL Player of the Month Award with this lead: "In the least surprising news of Wednesday …" The player would later say: "I feel like everything you win, you're actually doing it because of your teammates." Who was the AL Player of the Month for July 2017?

a) Yuli Gurriel
b) Carlos Correa
c) Jose Altuve
d) Alex Bregman

TOP OF THE THIRD ANSWER KEY

41: d. Roy Oswalt (2006).

42: a. George Springer.

43: d. Jake Marisnick.

44: d. Lance Berkman (2001).

45: b. Carlos Correa.

46: a. Lance McCullers.

47: b. Carlos Beltran.

48: d. 5 (he gave up only four earned runs in 34 innings of work ... all of which came on solo home runs).

49: b. Jose Altuve.

50: c. Jose Altuve.

BOTTOM OF THE THIRD

Q51: Hurricane Harvey devastated Houston in August 2017. The loss of life and property was catastrophic. The team's slogan became #HoustonStrong. A.J. Hinch said, "Athletes rarely need extra reasons to try to be great. But I think we've owned the responsibility of representing Houston the right way, and to be a stable part of a community that's going through something." Three weeks later the Astros clinched the division title, and in doing so, became the first team in major-league history to win titles in three different divisions—the NL Central, NL West, and AL West. It was the Astros' first division title since … when?
    a) 1986
    b) 1997
    c) 2001
    d) 2005

Q52: In Game 1 of the 2017 ALDS vs. the Boston Red Sox, this player hit three home runs—including two against Red Sox ace Chris Sale—to power the Astros to victory, 8-2. It was just the tenth postseason game in major-league history in which a player hit three home runs. Who had this extraordinary game?
    a) Evan Gattis
    b) Alex Bregman
    c) George Springer
    d) Jose Altuve

Q53: The Astros won Game 4 of the series on the road at Fenway, 5-4. Boston led 3-2 in the eighth, but then … who hit a game-tying home run for the Astros that sparked a come-from-behind victory?
    a) Evan Gattis

b) Alex Bregman
c) George Springer
d) Jose Altuve

Q54: And a follow-up … whose two-out single against closer Craig Kimbrel plated the go-ahead run?
a) Josh Reddick
b) Marwin Gonzalez
c) Yuli Gurriel
d) Carlos Correa

Q55: Houston faced the New York Yankees in the 2017 ALCS. The Astros won Game 1 at home, and then this pitcher took the mound for Game 2 … and tossed a complete game victory, 2-1. But the Yankees swept three straight in New York, and the Astros returned home for a win-or-go-home Game 6. Same pitcher … seven scoreless, 7-1 victory. Houston would go on to win the decisive Game 7, and for his two crucial victories this pitcher was named ALCS MVP. Who beat the Yankees twice to take home this prestigious honor?
a) Charlie Morton
b) Dallas Keuchel
c) Justin Verlander
d) Brad Peacock

Q56: Houston became the first team in major-league history to represent both leagues in the World Series—and the 2017 Series was the first since 1970 that featured two teams with 100 wins in the regular season (Houston 101, LA 104). LA won Game 1, 3-1. In Game 2, LA led 3-2 in the ninth … until this guy: Who hit a game-tying home run to set the stage for a dramatic extra-inning victory?
a) Evan Gattis
b) Marwin Gonzalez

c) Brian McCann

d) George Springer

Q57: And a follow-up … the Astros went on to hit three home runs in extra-innings. No other team in major-league history had ever done that in a postseason game—and no teammates had ever hit back-to-back extra-inning home runs in a World Series game until these guys: Which pair did this amazing feat in the 10th inning against the Dodgers?

    a) Evan Gattis/Brian McCann

    b) George Springer/Marwin Gonzalez

    c) Jose Altuve/Carlos Correa

    d) Yuli Gurriel/Alex Bregman

Q58: The hero of Game 3 vs. the Dodgers earned an 11-out save—a feat that had been achieved only twice previously in World Series history. He pitched 3 2/3 innings and gave up zero hits. And the save? It was the first of his career. Afterward, he would say: "It was awesome. I've never experienced anything like that in my life." Who came out of the pen to save Game 3 vs. the Dodgers?

    a) Collin McHugh

    b) Brad Peacock

    c) Lance McCullers

    d) Charlie Morton

Q59: LA won Game 4 to even the series—and then scored three first-inning runs against Dallas Keuchel in Game 5. In a truly historic game, the Astros became just the second team in major-league history to rally back from a three-run deficit *twice* in the same playoff game. LA led 4-0 in the fourth, and then the Astros scored four runs in the bottom of the frame. LA scored three in the top of the fifth, and then the Astros scored three in the home half of the fifth. Yuli Gurriel,

Jose Altuve, and LA's Cody Bellinger all hit three-run home runs. It was just the second time in major-league history that three different players homered with at least two runners on base during the same playoff game. Houston seemingly took control with four runs in the seventh and another in the eighth—but the Dodgers rallied back from their own three-run deficit in the ninth to send the game to extra-innings. And then this guy won it with a two-out single in the 10th … and became just the second player ever with at least one RBI in the first five World Series games of his career. Who was the hero in Game 5 vs. the Dodgers?

a) George Springer
b) Carlos Correa
c) Alex Bregman
d) Marwin Gonzalez

Q60: LA won Game 6, which made the Astros just the 10th team in baseball's divisional era to play a winner-take-all game in the LCS and the World Series in the same season. In Game 7, Houston scored five runs in the first two innings—including a two-run home run by the Series MVP—and then Charlie Morton came on in the sixth and pitched four innings of two-hit ball to close out the first World Series title in franchise history, 5-1. In the celebration that followed the victory, Jose Altuve said, "I caught the last out for the Houston Astros to become a world champion. It was a groundball to me, I threw to first, and I think it was the happiest moment of my life in baseball." Altuve—reflecting on the H Strong logos the Astros wore on their jerseys throughout the series—added, "I always believed that we could make it. We did this for them." Who won MVP honors after tying a World Series record with five home runs?

a) Jose Altuve
b) Alex Bregman

c) George Springer
d) Yuli Gurriel

BOTTOM OF THE THIRD ANSWER KEY

51: c. 2001.

52: d. Jose Altuve.

53: b. Alex Bregman.

54: a. Josh Reddick.

55: c. Justin Verlander.

56: b. Marwin Gonzalez.

57: c. Jose Altuve/Carlos Correa.

58: b. Brad Peacock.

59: c. Alex Bregman.

60: c. George Springer.

"Cheo [Jose Cruz] represents everything that's good about baseball, everything that's great about the Houston Astros."
— *David Medina, former Texas Supreme Court Judge*

4 FRANCHISE LEADERS

The Astros had some great moments in the latter years of the 20th century—but purists will always associate "20th century baseball" with teams like the Yankees, Red Sox, and Dodgers.

No worries.

It will be impossible to tell the story of 21st century major-league baseball without the Astros … because these guys are rewriting the record books.

Regular season. Postseason. It doesn't matter.

The biggest names in baseball?

They play for the Astros.

Here in the third, we explore some of the most significant franchise records and relive moments from some of the biggest names in the game.

TOP OF THE FOURTH

Q61: Jeff Bagwell retired with a franchise record 449 home runs and nine 30-homer seasons. His career high was 47. How many league home run titles did Bagwell win?
    a) 0
    b) 1
    c) 2
    d) 3

Q62: Jeff Bagwell holds numerous franchise records. This one is especially impressive because it speaks to his consistency. In how many consecutive seasons did Bagwell hit 30-plus home runs?
    a) 6
    b) 7
    c) 8
    d) 9

Q63: Only two of the top 10 home run leaders in franchise history are members of the 300-club. Bagwell, and this guy. Who is second in Astros history with 326 home runs?
    a) Craig Biggio
    b) Jimmy Wynn
    c) Lance Berkman
    d) Glenn Davis

Q64: Yordan Alvarez became just the fifth rookie in Astros history to hit 20-plus home runs … but did he set a franchise record? Which player hit a franchise record 27 home runs in his rookie season?
    a) Yordan Alvarez
    b) Carlos Correa

c) Lance Berkman

d) George Springer

Q65: Yordan Alvarez, Carlos Correa, Lance Berkman, and George Springer are four of the five players with 20-plus home runs as a rookie. The fifth player in this exclusive club was also the first to join it. Which player was the first rookie in franchise history to hit 20 home runs?

a) Jeff Bagwell
b) Hunter Pence
c) Glenn Davis
d) Craig Biggio

Q66: Only three players in franchise history had a career on-base percentage above .400. Whose .410 OBP is the highest career mark in Astros history?

a) Lance Berkman
b) Jeff Bagwell
c) Moises Alou
d) Bob Watson

Q67: This player set a franchise single-season record with 65 stolen bases. However, he was also thrown out attempting to steal a league high 27 times … which is also a franchise record. He's the only player in Astros history to be caught stealing 25 times in two different seasons. Who is this speedster?

a) Michael Bourn
b) Cesar Cedeno
c) Eric Yelding
d) Gerald Young

Q68: From 1962-2019, the Astros had four seasons in which a player hit 50-plus doubles: 1998, 1999, 2001, and 2018. Craig Biggio is easily the franchise career leader with 668 doubles—a total that ranks among the top 10 in major-league history, and through 2019 is the highest ever for a right-handed batter. However, does Biggio hold the Astros single-season record? Which player had a season in which he led the league with a franchise best 56 two-baggers?

a) Lance Berkman
b) Craig Biggio
c) Alex Bregman
d) Jose Altuve

Q69: J.R. Richard was the first pitcher in franchise history with double-digit strikeouts in five consecutive starts. He achieved the feat over two seasons from September 1979 through April 1980, and tallied 63 Ks in just 43 innings. That record was later obliterated by this guy. Who struck out 10-plus batters in a MLB record *nine* consecutive starts?

a) Nolan Ryan
b) Randy Johnson
c) Roy Oswalt
d) Gerrit Cole

Q70: The Astros hit three walk-off home runs in 2019. Michael Brantley, Yuli Gurriel, and Tony Kemp each had one. That total gave the club 98 walk-off home runs all-time, by 63 different batters. Who is the franchise leader with six career walk-off home runs?

a) Carlos Lee
b) Kevin Bass
c) Jose Cruz
d) Glenn Davis

TOP OF THE FOURTH ANSWER KEY

61: a. 0.

62: c. 8.

63: c. Lance Berkman.

64: a. Yordan Alvarez (2019).

65: c. Glenn Davis (1985).

66: a. Lance Berkman.

67: d. Gerald Young (1988).

68: b. Craig Biggio (1999).

69: d. Gerrit Cole (2019).

70: c. Jose Cruz.

BOTTOM OF THE FOURTH

Q71: A lot of speedsters suited up for the Astros throughout the years. Which one swiped a franchise record 487 bases?
 a) Gerald Young
 b) Billy Hatcher
 c) Craig Biggio
 d) Cesar Cedeno

Q72: This slugger had a season with a league-best 128 RBIs, and another season in which he set a franchise record with 136 RBIs (but was only third in the league in that category). Who was this prolific hitter?
 a) Jeff Bagwell
 b) Lance Berkman
 c) Carlos Lee
 d) Moises Alou

Q73: This pitcher set a franchise record with 18 strikeouts in a single-game. He beat Cincinnati 6-1, and gave up just five hits and two walks. Who holds this franchise record?
 a) Nolan Ryan
 b) Don Wilson
 c) Gerrit Cole
 d) J.R. Richard

Q74: This pitcher was the first 20-game winner in franchise history. He logged an impressive 305 1/3 innings while pitching 20 complete games. Who had this remarkable season?
 a) Don Wilson
 b) Denny Lemaster

c) Tom Griffin
d) Larry Dierker

Q75: This player set a franchise record with five pinch-hit home runs in a single-season. Who achieved this extraordinary feat?
a) Ollie Brown
b) Mike Easler
c) Cliff Johnson
d) Greg Gross

Q76: In today's game, a quality start for a pitcher is defined as six-plus innings with three or fewer earned runs allowed. If you apply that same standard to every guy who toed the rubber for the Astros, then who is the career leader in quality starts?
a) Roy Oswalt
b) Joe Niekro
c) Larry Dierker
d) Nolan Ryan

Q77: This pitcher had a season with 32 games started … and 32 quality starts. In 27 of 32 starts, he gave up two earned runs or less. He pitched 247 innings and never gave up more than three earned runs the entire season. Who had more quality starts in a single-season than any pitcher in franchise history?
a) J.R. Richard
b) Mike Scott
c) Don Wilson
d) Roy Oswalt

Q78: In 2008, Lance Berkman tied a franchise record when he scored at least one run in 15 consecutive games. Berkman was 29-for-57 with seven doubles, seven home runs, 17 RBIs, and 22 runs during that streak—and as a result, he won Player of the Week honors *twice* in a three-week span. Who was the *first* player in Astros history to score in 15 consecutive games?

a) Cesar Cedeno
b) Jose Cruz
c) Jeff Bagwell
d) Carlos Beltran

Q79: The franchise record for career grand slams is seven. Both Yuli Gurriel and George Springer—through 2019—have hit five. Whose record are Gurriel and Springer chasing?

a) Glenn Davis
b) Jeff Bagwell
c) Carlos Lee
d) Lance Berkman

Q80: This player had a season in which he batted .368 … but didn't win a batting title. However, he did establish a new franchise record for batting average. Who holds this record?

a) Moises Alou
b) Derek Bell
c) Rusty Staub
d) Jeff Bagwell

BOTTOM OF THE FOURTH ANSWER KEY

71: d. Cesar Cedeno.

72: b. Lance Berkman.

73: b. Don Wilson (July 14, 1968).

74: d. Larry Dierker (1969).

75: c. Cliff Johnson (1974).

76: c. Larry Dierker (206).

77: b. Mike Scott (1986).

78: d. Carlos Beltran (2004).

79: c. Carlos Lee.

80: d. Jeff Bagwell (1994).

"It's been a long time, you know. I'm not greedy, I'm not selfish, just wanted to go one time … it took us a long time and we've got five million people in Houston who are very pumped up right now."

— *Craig Biggio, 2005 NL Champion*

5 OCTOBER BASEBALL

"Next year" is the mentality that 29 of baseball's 30 teams cling to each winter, for there can be only one winner—as the 2019 Astros are painfully aware.

In the spring, the wins column is reset.

Last season is history.

And the goal is the same for every club: October baseball.

The journey is 162 games long, and the destination is a chance for baseball immortality. Let's take a look at the Astros in the playoffs.

TOP OF THE FIFTH

Q81: Jeff Bagwell reached base safely by hit or walk in 16 consecutive playoff games from 1999-2004. That streak was the longest in franchise history until 2019. Who broke Bagwell's record?
   a) Alex Bregman
   b) George Springer
   c) Michael Brantley
   d) Jose Altuve

Q82: The term "historic" is often overused. But it's entirely appropriate for describing Game 4 of the 2005 NLDS between the Astros and Braves. It was the first postseason game in history with two grand slams, the longest game in postseason history, and just the sixth time a series ended on a walk-off home run. Houston trailed by five runs in the eighth—but a Lance Berkman grand slam cut the deficit to one. And then in the ninth, with two outs, a guy with just three home runs in the regular season went deep to tie the game. Whose unexpected home run sent the game to extra-innings?
   a) Willy Taveras
   b) Brad Ausmus
   c) Adam Everett
   d) Jose Vizcaino

Q83: And a follow-up … the Astros won that marathon on a walk-off home run by a guy who entered the game as a pinch-runner. It was just the second time in postseason history that a pinch-runner stayed in the game and later hit a walk-off home run (Aaron Boone was the first in 2003). He would later reflect: "I'm just glad I could do my part. It was draining, mentally draining."
   a) Morgan Ensberg

b) Jason Lane
c) Luke Scott
d) Chris Burke

Q84: In 2015, Daniel Murphy—who hit just 14 home runs in the regular season for the New York Mets—set a MLB record when he homered in six consecutive games during a single postseason. The old record was five consecutive games. Which member of the Houston Astros previously held that record?
  a) Glenn Davis
  b) Jeff Bagwell
  c) Carlos Beltran
  d) Ken Caminiti

Q85: Lou Gehrig was the first player in MLB history to homer in four consecutive World Series games—but the games were over two years, 1928 and 1932. Reggie Jackson achieved the same feat in 1977 and 1978. A handful of players—most recently Barry Bonds in 2002—homered in three consecutive games during a single World Series. A member of the Houston Astros broke both records. He hit home runs in four consecutive games to conclude the 2017 World Series, and then homered in Game 1 of the 2019 World Series … thus making him the only player in MLB history to homer in four consecutive games during a single World Series and five consecutive World Series games overall in two different calendar years. Who achieved this remarkable feat?
  a) Jose Altuve
  b) Carlos Correa
  c) Alex Bregman
  d) George Springer

Q86: This player was the 11th in major-league history to clinch a postseason series with a walk-off home run. He would later say: "We're not going to the World Series because of me. We're going to the World Series because of everybody inside of the clubhouse." Who won the pennant with a home run?

a) George Springer
b) Jose Altuve
c) Carlos Correa
d) Alex Bregman

Q87: The first division title in franchise history was 1980. But that title nearly slipped away. Houston had a three-game lead, with three games to play. All three games were against the second place club … and Houston got swept. It forced a one-game playoff, and gave Joe Niekro a chance to be the hero. He took the mound and won his 20th game of the year and gave Houston its first-ever appearance in the playoffs. At that time it was the most important win in franchise history. Against which team—on the road, no less—did Joe Niekro deliver the game of his life?

a) Cincinnati Reds
b) Atlanta Braves
c) San Francisco Giants
d) Los Angeles Dodgers

Q88: The first-ever playoff game in Houston was Game 3 of the 1980 NLCS vs. Philadelphia. The game was scoreless through 10, but the Astros won it in the 11th on a sacrifice fly off the bat of Denny Walling. Who led off the 11th with a triple that set the stage for Walling's heroics?

a) Jose Cruz
b) Joe Morgan
c) Cesar Cedeno

d) Terry Puhl

Q89: And a follow-up … the other hero of that game was obviously the starting pitcher for the Astros. Who pitched 10 scoreless innings before finally giving way to the bullpen in the top of the 11th?
a) Joe Niekro
b) Nolan Ryan
c) Ken Forsch
d) J.R. Richard

Q90: Through 2019, the franchise record for most career quality starts in the postseason is eight. Who holds this record?
a) Roy Oswalt
b) Gerrit Cole
c) Justin Verlander
d) Brandon Backe

TOP OF THE FIFTH ANSWER KEY

81: d. Jose Altuve (25).

82: b. Brad Ausmus.

83: d. Chris Burke.

84: c. Carlos Beltran (2004).

85: d. George Springer.

86: b. Jose Altuve (2019).

87: d. Los Angeles Dodgers.

88: b. Joe Morgan.

89: a. Joe Niekro.

90: c. Justin Verlander.

BOTTOM OF THE FIFTH

Q91: Houston was second in the NL Central in 2005, finishing 11 games behind the St. Louis Cardinals. But with 89 wins, the Astros did enough to secure the wild-card. St. Louis was heavily favored to win the pennant—after all, it took just 82 wins for the San Diego Padres to claim the NL West, and 90 wins for the Atlanta Braves to claim the NL East. But the Astros stunned everyone—first eliminating the Braves in walk-off fashion, and then eliminating the Cardinals in six games for the first pennant in franchise history. The Series MVP made two starts, won both, and gave up just eight hits and two runs in 14 innings on the mound. Who beat the Cardinals twice to win 2005 NLCS MVP honors?

a) Roy Oswalt
b) Roger Clemens
c) Andy Pettitte
d) Brandon Backe

Q92: This pitcher was acquired by the Astros at the trade deadline and paid huge dividends in the Dog Days stretch run: 10-1, in just 11 starts. Houston was 37-16 after the trade, and ran away with the division title. Whose acquisition led to high hopes in October for Astros fans?

a) Justin Verlander
b) Randy Johnson
c) Zack Greinke
d) Jose Lima

Q93: This player hit safely in six consecutive at-bats during the playoffs ... *as a rookie*. Who set this major-league postseason record for rookies?

a) Yordan Alvarez
b) Alex Bregman
c) Yuli Gurriel
d) Kyle Tucker

Q94: Craig Biggio retired with a franchise record 39 postseason hits. That record has since been obliterated—thanks to an unprecedented streak of three consecutive 100-win seasons from 2017-19. Four players surpassed Biggio during that stretch: Yuli Gurriel, Carlos Correa, George Springer, and Jose Altuve. Which player closed out 2019 as the franchise leader for postseason hits?
a) Yuli Gurriel
b) Carlos Correa
c) George Springer
d) Jose Altuve

Q95: And a follow-up … in 2019, which player became the first in franchise history with two career walk-off hits in the postseason?
a) Yuli Gurriel
b) Carlos Correa
c) George Springer
d) Jose Altuve

Q96: The first postseason walk-off home run in Astros history was Game 1 of the 1981 NLDS. Nolan Ryan pitched nine innings and gave up just two hits—but Fernando Valenzuela was just as dominant for the Dodgers, and the score was tied, 1-1, in the bottom of the ninth. Then this guy … with two outs, who hit the Astros' first-ever postseason walk-off home run?
a) Art Howe
b) Jose Cruz
c) Phil Garner

d) Alan Ashby

Q97: In five seasons from 2015-19, George Springer hit a major-league high 15 postseason home runs. In fact, only four players had double-digit postseason home runs in that span—and all four played for the Astros: Springer, Jose Altuve, Carlos Correa, and Alex Bregman. It illustrates just how good the team was during that five-year stretch—four trips to the playoffs, via a wild-card berth and back-to-back-to-back 100-win seasons. Springer is currently—through 2019—the franchise leader in postseason home runs. The previous record was eight … and the crazy part? The guy who held it hit all eight *in a single postseason*. And yes, that's a major-league record. Who achieved this extraordinary feat?

a) Lance Berkman
b) Carlos Beltran
c) Mike Lamb
d) Jason Lane

Q98: This player hit a lead-off home run in Game 7 of the LCS. He's the only player in Astros history with a lead-off home run in the playoffs (through 2019). Who achieved this remarkable feat?

a) George Springer
b) Craig Biggio
c) Billy Hatcher
d) Jose Altuve

Q99: Lance Berkman is one of the all-time greats in Houston Astros history—and he was at his best in the playoffs. Berkman slashed .321/.426/.566 in 29 playoff games with the Astros—including six home runs, 26 RBIs, and 20 runs scored. His RBIs total was a franchise postseason record for more than a decade. However, from 2015-19, it was surpassed by four different players: Alex Bregman,

George Springer, Jose Altuve, and Carlos Correa. Which of those four established a new franchise record with 33 postseason RBIs?

a) Alex Bregman
b) George Springer
c) Jose Altuve
d) Carlos Correa

Q100: Brad Lidge appeared in 17 playoff games for the Astros. He saved a franchise best six playoff games, and his appearances were the most in club history until this guy … who made a franchise record 23 postseason appearances from 2015-19?

a) Justin Verlander
b) Will Harris
c) Ryan Pressly
d) Chad Qualls

BOTTOM OF THE FIFTH ANSWER KEY

91: a. Roy Oswalt.

92: b. Randy Johnson (1998).

93: c. Yuli Gurriel (2017).

94: d. Jose Altuve.

95: b. Carlos Correa.

96: d. Alan Ashby.

97: b. Carlos Beltran.

98: b. Craig Biggio (2004).

99: d. Carlos Correa.

100: b. Will Harris.

"Three thousand was something I wanted to accomplish this season. I honestly wrote off 300. I thought it was going to be a lot to ask for since these guys [Angels] don't strike out much."

— *Justin Verlander*

6 FANTASTIC FEATS

Fantastic feats are what draw us to the water cooler at work on Monday morning. "Did you see…?" is how the conversation begins. And inevitably it leads to stories about other guys, and more ridiculously impressive feats. Some fantastic feats are best told through numbers. Some defy any explanation at all. But all are worth sharing.

For example:

Justin Verlander began September 2019 with a no-hitter against the Blue Jays. It was his third career no-hitter, and his second on the road in Toronto.

Then, in his final start of the 2019 regular season, Justin Verlander struck out the Angels' Kole Calhoun for his 3,000th career strikeout—and he struck out Calhoun later in the same game for his 300th strikeout of 2019. In case you're curious, Verlander was just the 18th pitcher in history to reach 3,000 strikeouts, the 19th since 1900 to reach 300 in the same season—and only the second in major-league history to reach both milestones in the same game.

Fantastic, right?

Two more.

Verlander and Gerrit Cole became the first teammates in nearly two decades to record at least 300 strikeouts in the same season. And, Verlander had six games on the season with 12 or more strikeouts. That total was second in the league … behind Cole, who had nine such games, which was the highest total in baseball since Randy Johnson had 13 in 2001.

Here in the sixth, we look at some of the most fantastic feats from Houston Astros history.

TOP OF THE SIXTH

Q101: This player joined an elite club when he posted 30 home runs, 100 runs, and 100 RBIs … *in six consecutive seasons*. That's a feat fewer than 10 players in major-league history have accomplished. Who did this for the Astros?
 a) Lance Berkman
 b) Jeff Bagwell
 c) Richard Hidalgo
 d) Jimmy Wynn

Q102: This player was the first to hit a home run into the upper deck at the Astrodome. The ball traveled some 500 feet, and was hit against Hall of Fame knuckleballer Phil Niekro. Who achieved this remarkable feat?
 a) Jimmy Wynn
 b) Bob Watson
 c) Tommy Davis
 d) Jesus Alou

Q103: This player was the first in franchise history to reach 200 hits in a single-season. Who achieved this remarkable feat?
 a) Jose Altuve
 b) Moises Alou
 c) Craig Biggio
 d) Bob Watson

Q104: This player had an extraordinary stretch in which he had 200-plus hits in four consecutive seasons—and all four totals were best in the league. Who achieved this remarkable feat?
 a) Jose Altuve

b) Moises Alou
c) Craig Biggio
d) Bob Watson

Q105: Lee May was the first in franchise history to have a four-hit game six times during a single-season. Miguel Tejada was the second, when he achieved the feat in 2009. In 2016, who set a new franchise standard when he had eight such games?
a) George Springer
b) Michael Brantley
c) Carlos Correa
d) Jose Altuve

Q106: This player was the first—and through 2019, he remains the only—in franchise history to hit safely in 30 consecutive games. He batted .349 with 45 hits during the streak. Who achieved this extraordinary feat?
a) Hunter Pence
b) Willy Taveras
c) Jeff Kent
d) Moises Alou

Q107: Here's a fantastic feat for a coach: In 2014, he gave Jose Altuve three goals in Spring Training and then made a plan to obtain them: show more plate discipline, be an All-Star, and win a batting title. Altuve had just 53 strikeouts on the season, was an All-Star, and won the batting title. Nice job, coach. Which coach gets credit for these achievements?
a) Pat Listach
b) Bo Porter
c) John Mallee
d) Dave Trembley

Q108: The franchise record for reaching base safely is 52 consecutive games. It's been done twice. One player hit 11 home runs in his streak. The other hit … none. Streak still counts, though. Which two players share this franchise record?

    a) Jeff Bagwell/Craig Biggio
    b) Alex Bregman/Willy Taveras
    c) Jimmy Wynn/Greg Gross
    d) Lance Berkman/Joe Morgan

Q109: In 2019, both Yuli Gurriel and Jose Altuve had streaks in which they homered in five consecutive games (and both hit six home runs in their respective five-game streaks). The Astros had only three such streaks in the previous 57 seasons in franchise history. Who is the only member of the Houston Astros to hit a home run in *six* consecutive games?

    a) Morgan Ensberg
    b) Cliff Johnson
    c) Lance Berkman
    d) Jeff Bagwell

Q110: One player had 15 separate streaks in which he homered in three or more consecutive games for the Houston Astros. That's astounding. Which slugger achieved this feat?

    a) Glenn Davis
    b) Jimmy Wynn
    c) Jeff Bagwell
    d) Lance Berkman

TOP OF THE SIXTH ANSWER KEY

101: b. Jeff Bagwell (1996-2001).

102: a. Jimmy Wynn (1970).

103: c. Craig Biggio (1998).

104: a. Jose Altuve (2014-17).

105: d. Jose Altuve.

106: b. Willy Taveras (2006).

107: c. John Mallee (hitting coach).

108: c. Jimmy Wynn (1969, 11 HR)/Greg Gross (1975, 0 HR).

109: a. Morgan Ensberg (April 2006).

110: d. Lance Berkman.

BOTTOM OF THE SIXTH

Q111: This player set a franchise record when he had at least one RBI in 10 consecutive games. They weren't cheap, either. He batted .405 with 15 hits, seven home runs, and 19 RBIs. Who achieved this remarkable feat?
   a) Lance Berkman
   b) Bob Watson
   c) Chris Carter
   d) Jose Cruz

Q112: Any no-hit game is special. However, this pitcher tossed a no-hitter *and* clinched a division title in the same game. Who achieved this extraordinary feat?
   a) Nolan Ryan
   b) Ken Forsch
   c) Mike Scott
   d) Darryl Kile

Q113: In Houston Astros history (through 2019), ten different pitchers have won 20 games in a season. Who set a franchise record with 22 wins?
   a) Roy Oswalt
   b) Dallas Keuchel
   c) Mike Hampton
   d) Larry Dierker

Q114: This pitcher was the first in franchise history to win 20 games in two different seasons. Who achieved this remarkable feat?
   a) Roy Oswalt
   b) Joe Niekro

c) Mike Hampton
d) Mike Scott

Q115: Gerrit Cole set a franchise record with 10 or more strikeouts in 21 games during the 2019 regular season. He was the first pitcher in nearly two decades—since Randy Johnson in 2001—with more than 20 such games in a season. Who held the previous Astros' single-season record with 10 or more strikeouts in 14 games?
  a) Nolan Ryan
  b) Randy Johnson
  c) Roy Oswalt
  d) J.R. Richard

Q116: Jeff Bagwell had eight seasons with 30 home runs, 100 RBIs, and 100 runs. Only seven players in MLB history—including legends such as Babe Ruth and Jimmie Foxx—had more than eight 30/100/100 seasons. Alex Rodriguez holds the MLB record with 12. Who was the first player in Astros history with 30 home runs, 100 RBIs, and 100 runs in a single-season?
  a) Jeff Bagwell
  b) Jimmy Wynn
  c) Moises Alou
  d) Richard Hidalgo

Q117: In today's game it seems like everyone can hit home runs and no one worries about striking out. It hasn't always been this way. It's true that historically power hitters tended to strike out more than most—but it's never been as endemic as it is now. In the 2018 and 2019 seasons, only three MLB players had a season with 30 home runs while striking out fewer times than they walked. Jose Ramirez did it for the Indians in 2018, and his teammate Carlos Santana did it in 2019. Then this guy … he did it in *both* seasons for the Astros.

Who achieved this extraordinary feat?

a) Yuli Gurriel
b) Jose Altuve
c) Alex Bregman
d) George Springer

Q118: The first-ever Astrodome no-hitter was on June 18, 1967. It featured 15 Ks—including Hank Aaron to end the game. Which pitcher is in the history books for this extraordinary game?

a) Larry Dierker
b) Don Wilson
c) Mike Cuellar
d) Bo Belinsky

Q119: This pitcher was the first modern era right-hander in NL history with 300 strikeouts in a single-season. Who achieved this remarkable feat?

a) Don Wilson
b) J.R. Richard
c) Nolan Ryan
d) Tom Griffin

Q120: In 2010, Jason Heyward hit an Opening Day home run for the Atlanta Braves. In 2011, he did it again. The 21-year-old outfielder became the youngest player in major-league history to achieve that feat in consecutive seasons. The third youngest player in major-league history to hit Opening Day home runs in consecutive seasons did so for the Houston Astros. Who achieved this remarkable feat?

a) Alex Bregman
b) Jose Altuve
c) Carlos Correa

d) George Springer

BOTTOM OF THE SIXTH ANSWER KEY

111: a. Lance Berkman.

112: c. Mike Scott (1986).

113: c. Mike Hampton (1999).

114: b. Joe Niekro (1979, 1980).

115: d. J.R. Richard (1978, and again in 1979).

116: b. Jimmy Wynn (1967).

117: c. Alex Bregman.

118: b. Don Wilson.

119: b. J.R. Richard (1978).

120: c. Carlos Correa (2016-17, ages 21 and 22).

"I was never that great. But something my father instilled in me when I was a kid is to never quit. Don't quit at anything you ever try … deep inside of me, I just never gave up. I continued to get a little bit better every year, and that drive that my mom and my father gave me got me a long way."

— *Jeff Bagwell, Hall of Fame speech*

7 AWARD WINNERS

Whitey Herzog famously said, "We need just two players to be a contender: Babe Ruth and Sandy Koufax."

It's a funny line.

It also underscores a significant truth: baseball is a team game. Even Herzog, in his jest, said *contender*. If you want to be a champion, then you need a team. You don't build a franchise as successful as the Astros unless the franchise culture embraces that simple fact.

But, the hardware *is* nice.

In the seventh, the trivia is all about award-winning Astros.

TOP OF THE SEVENTH

Q121: This player won the Rookie of the Year Award, and later in his career he won the Most Valuable Player Award. He was the first player in Astros history to claim both awards. Who achieved this remarkable feat?
  a) Jose Altuve
  b) Jeff Bagwell
  c) Craig Biggio
  d) Glenn Davis

Q122: This player was the first in franchise history to win a batting title. He began play on the season's final day with a three-point lead in the title race and could have sat the bench to protect the narrow advantage. He chose to play and went 2-for-4 to secure the title. His manager would later say: "That caps off [who he is] as a person, the hard work he put in. He went out and finished the job. He did it on the field." Who won the first batting title in franchise history?
  a) Craig Biggio
  b) Jose Altuve
  c) Jose Cruz
  d) Moises Alou

Q123: This pitcher was the first in franchise history to win the Cy Young Award. He won 18 games and led the majors in innings pitched (275 1/3), strikeouts (306), and ERA (2.22). Who is this award-winning pitcher?
  a) Don Wilson
  b) Mike Scott
  c) Roy Oswalt
  d) J.R. Richard

Q124: He guided the Astros to 93 wins and a division title—and won the first Manager of the Year Award in franchise history. Which manager achieved this feat?
   a) Bill Virdon
   b) Hal Lanier
   c) Larry Dierker
   d) A.J. Hinch

Q125: The Roberto Clemente Award is one of the most prestigious honors in baseball. It is given to the player "who demonstrates the values Hall of Famer Roberto Clemente displayed in his commitment to community and understanding the value of helping others" (MLB.com). Only one player from across MLB receives the annual award. Who is the only player in Astros history (through 2019) to receive this honor?
   a) Roy Oswalt
   b) Bob Watson
   c) Shane Reynolds
   d) Craig Biggio

Q126: This third baseman was the first player in Astros history to win a Gold Glove. He's also the only player in team history to win five consecutive Gold Gloves at any position. Who achieved both of these remarkable feats?
   a) Enos Cabell
   b) Doug Rader
   c) Phil Garner
   d) Bob Aspromonte

Q127: The Players Choice Awards are given annually to the outstanding player, rookie, pitcher, and comeback player in each league—as voted on anonymously by the players (MLB.com). Who was the first rookie in Astros history to be given this honor by his MLB peers?

    a) Willy Taveras
    b) Carlos Correa
    c) Lance Berkman
    d) Roy Oswalt

Q128: The Hank Aaron Award is given annually to the "best overall offensive performer in both leagues" (MLB.com). Fans get to vote on this award—as does Hank Aaron himself, along with a panel of Hall of Fame legends. Who was the first player in Astros history to win the Hank Aaron Award?

    a) Jeff Bagwell
    b) Jose Altuve
    c) Craig Biggio
    d) Lance Berkman

Q129: This fan-favorite was the first in Astros history to win a Players Choice Award for Outstanding Player. Who received this honor?

    a) Jeff Bagwell
    b) Jose Altuve
    c) Craig Biggio
    d) Alex Bregman

Q130: This player was the first in Astros history to win a Players Choice Award for Outstanding Pitcher. Who received this honor?

    a) Roy Oswalt
    b) Roger Clemens
    c) Dallas Keuchel
    d) Mike Hampton

TOP OF THE SEVENTH ANSWER KEY

121: b. Jeff Bagwell (1991, 1994).

122: b. Jose Altuve (.341 in 2014; quote attributed to interim manager Tom Lawless).

123: b. Mike Scott (1986).

124: a. Bill Virdon (1980).

125: d. Craig Biggio (2007).

126: b. Doug Rader (1970-74).

127: a. Willy Taveras (2005).

128: b. Jose Altuve (2017).

129: a. Jeff Bagwell (1994).

130: d. Mike Hampton (1999).

BOTTOM OF THE SEVENTH

Q131: This player won the All-Star Game with an extra-inning home run—and as a result, he became the first Astros player in history to win MVP honors in the Midsummer Classic. Who achieved this remarkable feat?
 a) George Springer
 b) Glenn Davis
 c) Alex Bregman
 d) Jose Cruz

Q132: In 2014, the awards for top relievers in each league were renamed after Mariano Rivera and Trevor Hoffman—the most successful closers in baseball history. From 1976-2012, the top reliever in each league won the Relief Man Award. Who won the only Relief Man Award in Astros history?
 a) Dave Smith
 b) Brad Lidge
 c) Jose Valverde
 d) Billy Wagner

Q133: Houston's 2019 pennant was the third in franchise history (2005, 2017). Who was the first position player to win LCS MVP honors for the Astros?
 a) Craig Biggio
 b) Morgan Ensberg
 c) George Springer
 d) Jose Altuve

Q134: Only once in franchise history has a pitcher won 15 home games during the regular season. In 18 starts, he was 15-0, with a

1.46 ERA and 139 strikeouts in 129 1/3 innings. Which award-winning pitcher posted these record-setting numbers?
a) Roger Clemens
b) Dallas Keuchel
c) Mike Scott
d) Justin Verlander

Q135: In 2019, Yordan Alvarez became just the third rookie in major-league history to hit more than 25 home runs in 100 games or fewer—Tony Clark (1996) and Trevor Story (2016) were the others, but neither Clark nor Story won ROY honors. Alvarez did. Unanimously. Alvarez began the season on fire at Triple-A Round Rock. He debuted with the Astros on June 9, and immediately hit a home run against the Orioles. If you combine his Round Rock stats with what he did for the Astros … how many home runs did Alvarez hit across two levels of pro ball in 2019?
a) 45
b) 50
c) 55
d) 60

Q136: Yordan Alvarez spent just four months in the big leagues in 2019. How many times did he win AL Rookie of the Month honors?
a) 1
b) 2
c) 3
d) 4

Q137: This player slashed .360/.405/.620, with six home runs and 20 RBIs in 27 games—and became the first player in franchise history to win the NL Player of the Month Award. Who achieved this feat?

a) Bob Watson
b) Jose Cruz
c) Art Howe
d) Kevin Bass

Q138: This player was the first in Astros history to win the Pitcher of the Month Award three times … and he won all three in a single-season. Who is this award-winning pitcher?
a) Mike Scott
b) Roy Oswalt
c) Dallas Keuchel
d) Justin Verlander

Q139: This player was the first in franchise history to win an ESPY. He won for Breakthrough Athlete of the Year. Who achieved this honor?
a) Craig Biggio
b) Jeff Bagwell
c) Jose Altuve
d) Carlos Correa

Q140: The Lou Gehrig Memorial Award recognizes players who "exhibit the character and integrity of Lou Gehrig" (MLB.com). It's a prestigious honor, and the list of recipients includes many of baseball's biggest names. In 1988, Buddy Bell was the first player in Astros history to win the award. Glenn Davis was the second when he won it just two years later. Who is the most recent player (through 2019) in Astros history to win the Lou Gehrig Memorial Award?
a) Jeff Bagwell
b) Craig Biggio
c) Jose Altuve
d) Lance McCullers

BOTTOM OF THE SEVENTH ANSWER KEY

131: c. Alex Bregman (2018).

132: d. Billy Wagner (1999).

133: d. Jose Altuve (2019).

134: b. Dallas Keuchel (2015 Cy Young Award).

135: b. 50 (.324, 50 HR, 149 RBIs, 143 G).

136: c. 3 (June, July, August).

137: a. Bob Watson (May 1972).

138: c. Dallas Keuchel (April, May, and August 2015).

139: b. Jeff Bagwell (1995).

140: c. Jose Altuve (2016).

"You know what, Houston? You're a championship city."
— *A.J. Hinch*

8 THE TEAMS

As we move to the eighth, we take a look at some of the greatest players and moments in Astros history through the lens of *teams*. An opponent, year, or even a college—the answers are team-centered: From the first game in franchise history through the record-setting power of the 2019 Astros.

Prolific offenses?

Dominant pitching?

Ridiculously long games?

Snarky scoreboards?

All here in the eighth. Let's get started.

TOP OF THE EIGHTH

Q141: Four sluggers hit 30-plus home runs for the 2019 Astros: Jose Altuve, Alex Bregman, Yuli Gurriel, and George Springer. This remarkable achievement was a franchise first. Only one previous club had as many as three 30-homer seasons. For which club did Moises Alou, Jeff Bagwell, and Richard Hidalgo all hit 30-plus home runs?
   a) 1997
   b) 1998
   c) 1999
   d) 2000

Q142: The expansion Houston Colt .45s began play in 1962 at the mosquito-infested Colt Stadium. The roster was made up from the expansion draft that took place in October 1961. In that draft, the Colt .45s had the first overall pick and selected an infielder from the San Francisco Giants … but a month later, the club traded him to the Boston Red Sox. Who never played an inning for the Colt .45s despite being their first pick in the expansion draft?
   a) Don Buddin
   b) Eddie Bressoud
   c) Dave Roberts
   d) Ernie Fazio

Q143: Craig Biggio only had a partial scholarship to play college baseball. He went on to become a first-round draft pick. For which team did Biggio play collegiately?
   a) University of Arkansas
   b) Pepperdine University
   c) Seton Hall University
   d) Mississippi State University

Q144: Jeff Bagwell was a diehard Red Sox fan who grew up in the northeast—but he had almost no options to continue his career past high school. For which team did Bagwell finally earn a shot at playing college ball?
   a) Amherst College
   b) Clark University
   c) Bates College
   d) University of Hartford

Q145: The first game in franchise history was April 10, 1962. The Houston Colt .45s won that game 11-2. Which team was Houston's opponent in that inaugural game?
   a) Chicago Cubs
   b) Cincinnati Reds
   c) Pittsburgh Pirates
   d) Milwaukee Braves

Q146: The first-ever indoor baseball game was an exhibition between the Astros and Yankees. Houston won it, 2-1. In the regular season that followed, Joe Morgan set Houston records for at-bats, runs, hits, and triples. And in that same season … the Colt .45s officially became the Astros. In which season did all this take place?
   a) 1964
   b) 1965
   c) 1966
   d) 1967

Q147: In a season referred to in historical terms as the "Year of the Pitcher," the Astros and Mets played the longest 1-0 game in baseball history. Don Wilson pitched nine scoreless for the Astros. Tom Seaver pitched 10 scoreless for the Mets. The Astros' scoreboard flashed a message in the 20th inning that read: "We hope you are enjoying tonight's third game as much as you enjoyed the first two." The Astros won in 24 innings when a routine groundball off the bat of Bob Aspromonte went through the legs of Mets shortstop Al Weis. In which season did this historic game occur?

    a) 1966
    b) 1967
    c) 1968
    d) 1969

Q148: The Astros played consecutive no-hit games on April 30 and May 1, 1969. The club was no-hit on April 30, but on May 1—against the very same opponent—Don Wilson pitched his second career no-hitter. It was just the second time in history that opponents no-hit each other on consecutive days. Against which opponent did the Astros make history?

    a) Atlanta Braves
    b) Cincinnati Reds
    c) Los Angeles Dodgers
    d) San Francisco Giants

Q149: The Colt .45s won just 64 games during their inaugural 1962 season—and it didn't improve for a long time. In which season did the Houston Astros finally achieve a .500 record?

    a) 1968
    b) 1969
    c) 1970
    d) 1971

Q150: Houston played its home games at the Astrodome for the better part of four decades. Only twice did the club score 800 runs in a season: 1998 and 1999. The new ballpark opened in 2000, and that club immediately obliterated the franchise record 874 runs scored by the 1998 Astros. In 20 seasons at Minute Maid Park through 2019, the Astros scored 800 runs four times and 900 runs twice. Which club is the highest scoring in franchise history with 938 runs?

    a) 2000
    b) 2003
    c) 2017
    d) 2019

TOP OF THE EIGHTH ANSWER KEY

141: d. 2000.

142: b. Eddie Bressoud.

143: c. Seton Hall University.

144: d. University of Hartford.

145: a. Chicago Cubs.

146: b. 1965.

147: c. 1968.

148: b. Cincinnati Reds.

149: b. 1969 (81-81).

150: a. 2000.

BOTTOM OF THE EIGHTH

Q151: The 2019 Astros hit an astounding 288 home runs—which shattered the previous franchise single-season record of 249—and yet, the club was one home run shy of something truly historic. Alex Bregman led the 2019 Astros with 41 home runs. George Springer hit 39. Had Springer gone yard once more during the regular season, then it would have been just the second time in franchise history that the Astros had a pair of 40-homer guys in a single-season. Which team was the first—and so far, only—to achieve this remarkable feat?
  a) 1999
  b) 2000
  c) 2015
  d) 2018

Q152: In Houston's first 58 seasons, only three times did the club produce three 15-game winners in a single-season. The first trio of pitchers to achieve this feat was Pete Harnisch, Darryl Kile, and Mark Portugal. In which season did those three pitchers all win 15-plus games?
  a) 1992
  b) 1993
  c) 1994
  d) 1995

Q153: And a follow-up … which trio of pitchers is the most recent to all win 15-plus games in a single-season?
  a) Collin McHugh, Mike Fiers, Dallas Keuchel
  b) Lance McCullers, Doug Fister, Dallas Keuchel
  c) Gerrit Cole, Charlie Morton, Justin Verlander
  d) Charlie Morton, Dallas Keuchel, Mike Fiers

Q154: In Houston's first 58 seasons, only twice has the club produced three pitchers with 200-plus strikeouts in a single-season. Larry Dierker, Tom Griffin, and Don Wilson achieved this feat in 1969. Which trio is the most recent to accomplish this remarkable feat?
   a) Collin McHugh, Mike Fiers, Dallas Keuchel
   b) Lance McCullers, Doug Fister, Dallas Keuchel
   c) Gerrit Cole, Charlie Morton, Justin Verlander
   d) Charlie Morton, Dallas Keuchel, Mike Fiers

Q155: From 1931-33, the New York Yankees scored at least one run in a major-league record 308 consecutive games. Only two other franchises can boast a streak of 200 games or more without being shutout: Milwaukee and Cincinnati. The longest streak in Astros history is 122 games over two seasons. In which seasons did the Astros play 122 games without being shutout?
   a) 2000-01
   b) 2001-02
   c) 2016-17
   d) 2017-18

Q156: Houston beat Oakland 15-0 on September 9, 2019—and in that game the Astros tied a franchise record with seven home runs. Which club was the first in Astros history to hit seven home runs in a game (a 14-4 victory vs. the Cubs)?
   a) 1997
   b) 1998
   c) 1999
   d) 2000

Q157: And a follow-up … the Astros had only 14 games in 58 seasons in which the club hit six or more home runs. One club had a franchise record four such games in a single-season. Which team set this record?

a) 1999
b) 2000
c) 2018
d) 2019

Q158: The Astros have won 100 games four times in 58 seasons—including three consecutive from 2017-19. Which team was the first in franchise history to win 100 games?

a) 1998
b) 2001
c) 2003
d) 2005

Q159: This club endured the longest road trip in Astros history—26 days—because the Astrodome was being used for the Republican National Convention. Which club spent nearly a month on the road?

a) 1984
b) 1988
c) 1992
d) 1996

Q160: In 1995, MLB expanded the playoffs to include a wild-card team in each league. Led by team MVP Craig Biggio, the Astros were one-game back in the wild-card chase on the season's final day. The Astros had to beat the Cubs, and then needed some help from the San Francisco Giants to force a one-game playoff for the wild-card berth. The Astros did their part, 8-7, on the road at Wrigley Field. And when the Giants scored eight runs in three innings it looked as if they might do their part as well. But the Giants blew it, 10-9, and the Astros came up one game short in the first-ever wild-card chase …

behind which team?
  a) Cincinnati Reds
  b) Los Angeles Dodgers
  c) Colorado Rockies
  d) San Diego Padres

BOTTOM OF THE EIGHTH ANSWER KEY

151: b. 2000 (Jeff Bagwell, Richard Hidalgo).

152: b. 1993.

153: c. Gerrit Cole, Charlie Morton, Justin Verlander (2018).

154: c. Gerrit Cole, Charlie Morton, Justin Verlander (2018).

155: b. 2001-02.

156: d. 2000.

157: b. 2000.

158: a. 1998.

159: c. 1992.

160: c. Colorado Rockies.

"Historically ... people would look at the past and they would project the future by just dragging out the past. That is just not the right way to do it. The data available today has made it better and easier to forecast the future."

— *Abraham Wyner, host of Wharton Moneyball*

9 ANALYTICS

There are distinct eras in baseball history precisely because the game evolves with time. However, you could argue it's the evolution of data—or more precisely, how we manipulate, extract, and interpret data—that is the driving force behind today's game. Statistics professor Abraham Wyner calls it "the new norm" that teams will use analytics to build rosters, offer contracts, and evaluate prospects.

Diehard fans are on board as well.

FanGraphs and Baseball-Reference are must-use sites for fanatics. The debates that rage on social media are epic. The ability to interact with athletes, executives, and like-minded fans on platforms such as Twitter only drives fans to delve deeper into data.

It really is "the new norm."

And here in the ninth, it's the source for our trivia.

TOP OF THE NINTH

Q161: Batting Average on Balls in Play (BABIP)—this stat excludes home runs, and measures how often a batted ball goes for a hit (FanGraphs.com). It can tell you if a player is successful (or not) due to talent, defense, or luck. The logic behind it suggests hitters have more control over batted ball outcomes than do pitchers. Which player led the Astros with a .366 BABIP in 2019?
   a) Michael Brantley
   b) Jose Altuve
   c) Alex Bregman
   d) Yordan Alvarez

Q162: Isolated Power (ISO)—measures raw power as the ratio of extra bases per at-bat, and reveals how often a player hits for extra bases (FanGraphs.com). It better reflects the type of hitter you are evaluating than does traditional batting average or slugging percentage. Which player led the Astros with a .342 ISO in 2019?
   a) Michael Brantley
   b) Jose Altuve
   c) Alex Bregman
   d) Yordan Alvarez

Q163: Weighted On-Base Average (wOBA)—developed by Tom Tango (*The Book: Playing the Percentages in Baseball*), it is used to measure overall offensive value using the relative values of distinct offensive events (FanGraphs.com). In short, it means a traditional stat such as batting average weights all hits equally, while slugging percentage weights hits based on total bases, as if a double is twice as valuable as a single. The point of wOBA is to weight all aspects of hitting in proportion to their actual run value. FanGraphs, as a general rule for wOBA, considers .400 excellent while .320 is average. Which player led the Astros with a .435 wOBA in 2019?

    a) Michael Brantley

    b) Jose Altuve

    c) Alex Bregman

    d) Yordan Alvarez

Q164: Weighted Runs Above Average (wRAA)—in simple terms, this stat tells us the number of runs a player contributes to his team when compared to an average player. A wRAA of zero indicates an average player. FanGraphs, as a general rule for wRAA, considers 10 as above average, 20 as great, and 40 as excellent. In 2019, Mike Trout led the AL with 60.4 wRAA—while the Astros had six players above 20. Which player led the Astros and was second in the league with 58.8 wRAA?

    a) Michael Brantley

    b) Jose Altuve

    c) Alex Bregman

    d) Yordan Alvarez

Q165: Wins Above Replacement (WAR)—in simple terms, WAR seeks to answer this question: How many wins does a player add to his team compared with what a replacement player would add? It was developed by Sean Smith and is calculated in different ways depending on your preferred database. Cody Bellinger led MLB with 9.0 WAR in 2019. Which player led the Astros and was second in baseball with 8.4 WAR?

    a) Michael Brantley

    b) Jose Altuve

    c) Alex Bregman

    d) Yordan Alvarez

Q166: Using the Baseball-Reference WAR for position players, in general terms, five represents All-Star quality while eight is an MVP-caliber season. Which player had 9.4 WAR during a season in which he placed fourth in MVP balloting?
   a) Jeff Bagwell
   b) Glenn Davis
   c) Jose Altuve
   d) Craig Biggio

Q167: WAR can be separated out by offense and defense as well. dWAR uses only defensive stats. Using this Baseball-Reference metric, Andrelton Simmons had 5.5 dWAR for the Atlanta Braves in 2013—a number that ranks highest in MLB history through 2019. The best dWAR in Astros history currently ranks among the top 20 in baseball history as well. Who achieved 4.1 dWAR in 2006?
   a) Eric Bruntlett
   b) Adam Everett
   c) Morgan Ensberg
   d) Willy Taveras

Q168: Exit velocity "measures the speed of a baseball as it comes off the bat, immediately after a batter makes contact" (MLB.com). It can be used to evaluate hitters and pitchers. A high exit velocity increases the odds that a Batted Ball Event (BBE) will be positive—for the hitter, not so much if you're the pitcher. The highest exit velocity of 2019 came off the bat of Giancarlo Stanton—120.6 mph. How far did it go? Well, 279 feet. As singles go, that's not bad. The highest exit velocity for the Astros in 2019 was actually a 117.9 mph out. Who had the highest exit velocity of the season for the Astros?
   a) Alex Bregman
   b) George Springer

c) Jose Altuve

d) Yordan Alvarez

Q169: The longest home run hit by the Astros during the 2019 regular season was 474 feet. Two different players achieved this feat. One had an exit velocity of 111.5 mph and a launch angle of 28 to straightaway center off a 90.5 mph 4-seam fastball—the other had an exit velocity of 112.2 mph and a launch angle of 24 to right field off a 91.2 mph 4-seam fastball. Which duo smashed those fastballs 474 feet?

a) Carlos Correa/Yordan Alvarez

b) Jose Altuve/Michael Brantley

c) George Springer/Yuli Gurriel

d) Alex Bregman/Kyle Tucker

Q170: We already defined "late and close" as "the seventh inning or later with the hitter's team tied, ahead by one, or has the tying run on base, at bat, or on deck" (MLB.com). This stat falls under the much debated "clutch" category. Which player had a franchise record 41 late and close hits in a single-season?

a) Gerald Young

b) Jose Cruz

c) Derek Bell

d) Miguel Tejada

TOP OF THE NINTH ANSWER KEY

161: d. Yordan Alvarez.

162: d. Yordan Alvarez.

163: d. Yordan Alvarez (it should be noted that Alvarez had only 369 plate appearances, whereas Alex Bregman had 690 with a wOBA of .418).

164: c. Alex Bregman.

165: c. Alex Bregman.

166: d. Craig Biggio (1997).

167: b. Adam Everett.

168: d. Yordan Alvarez.

169: a. Carlos Correa (111.5, 28, 90.5)/Yordan Alvarez (112.2, 24, 91.2).

170: c. Derek Bell (1998).

BOTTOM OF THE NINTH

Q171: The Astros made the playoffs four times in five seasons from 2015-19. This player had 49 defensive runs saved (DRS) in that span. The second highest total on the club was just 22. DRS measures the number of runs a player is better or worse on defense relative to an average player. The higher the number, the more runs saved. Whose defense most impacted the Astros' won-loss record from 2015-19?
   a) George Springer
   b) Josh Reddick
   c) Jake Marisnick
   d) Carlos Correa

Q172: Ultimate Zone Rating (UZR)—one of the most widely used defensive statistics, UZR assigns a run value to defense in an attempt to quantify how many runs a player saved or gave up in the field (FanGraphs.com). Typically it is considered more reliable when used with data that spans multiple seasons—however, which outfielder had the highest UZR for the 2019 Astros?
   a) Jake Marisnick
   b) Josh Reddick
   c) Michael Brantley
   d) George Springer

Q173: Total Zone Runs (TZR)—this Baseball-Reference metric is similar to UZR, as it measures total fielding runs above average, based on the number of plays made (Baseball-Reference.com). Who is the most recent Astros player (through 2019) to lead the league in TZR?
   a) Jake Marisnick
   b) Carlos Gomez
   c) Dexter Fowler

d) Michael Bourn

Q174: Fielding Independent Pitching (FIP)—it is a number similar to ERA, however, "it focuses solely on the events a pitcher has the most control over: strikeouts, unintentional walks, hit-by-pitches, and home runs" (MLB.com). The idea is to eliminate results on balls in play, because a pitcher has no control over their outcome—and for that reason, FIP is often considered a better metric than ERA for determining a pitcher's effectiveness. For example, you can have a low FIP and a high ERA—which would indicate bad luck on balls in play, and a guy you don't want to give up on. If you apply FIP throughout Astros history ... then who produced a franchise best 1.94 FIP for a single-season?
 a) J.R. Richard
 b) Mike Scott
 c) Nolan Ryan
 d) Jim Deshaies

Q175: And a follow-up ... among pitchers with at least 500 innings, who has the lowest career FIP in Astros history?
 a) Nolan Ryan
 b) J.R. Richard
 c) Mike Cuellar
 d) Roy Oswalt

Q176: Adjusted Earned Run Average (ERA+)—this normalizes a pitcher's ERA by accounting "for external factors like ballparks and opponents" (MLB.com). A score of 100 is the league average, so a score of 150 is 50% better than the league average. Among pitchers with 500 innings, whose career 180 ERA+ is the best all-time in Astros history?
 a) Billy Wagner

b) Roger Clemens
c) Andy Pettitte
d) Mike Hampton

Q177: Wins Above Replacement (WAR)—this time for pitchers; it adjusts FIP for factors such as league and ballpark, and then uses league averages to determine "how many wins a pitcher was worth based on those numbers and his innings pitched total" (MLB.com). Which pitcher has the highest career WAR in Astros history?
a) Nolan Ryan
b) Mike Scott
c) Roy Oswalt
d) J.R. Richard

Q178: And a follow-up … Justin Verlander had 7.8 WAR during his 2019 Cy Young season. If you apply modern metrics to stars from the past, you truly begin to understand how analytics has changed our interpretation of what individual players contribute to the team. The Astros' season record for pitching WAR is 8.6—by a guy who didn't get a single Cy Young vote. Which pitcher had this historic season?
a) Nolan Ryan
b) Mike Scott
c) Larry Dierker
d) Gerrit Cole

Q179: Win Probability Added (WPA)—this is an event-based stat, that measures "the importance of a given plate appearance in the context of the game" (MLB.com). If you hit a grand slam, it's pretty awesome—but if you hit it after your team already has a 10-run lead, then it's not worth nearly as much as a solo home run when your team is trailing by a run. Hence, the context factor. The actual measurement is the probability your at-bat adds to or detracts from your team's odds of winning an individual game. Whose career 59.4 WPA is the highest in franchise history?

a) Lance Berkman
b) Craig Biggio
c) Jeff Bagwell
d) Jim Wynn

Q180: And a follow-up … Alex Bregman had 5.8 WPA in 2018, and 4.0 WPA in 2019—both totals led the club. Who holds this franchise record with 7.2 WPA in a single-season?

a) Glenn Davis
b) Jose Cruz
c) Billy Hatcher
d) Cesar Cedeno

BOTTOM OF THE NINTH ANSWER KEY

171: c. Jake Marisnick.

172: d. George Springer.

173: d. Michael Bourn (2010).

174: a. J.R. Richard (1980).

175: c. Mike Cuellar (2.39).

176: b. Roger Clemens.

177: c. Roy Oswalt.

178: c. Larry Dierker (1969).

179: c. Jeff Bagwell.

180: d. Cesar Cedeno (1972).

"We were like two tired old men walking out of the tunnel, and then we were like two kids having a good time."

— *Roger Clemens, on teammate Craig Biggio, after the Astros beat the Braves in 18 innings to win the 2005 NLDS*

10 EXTRA INNINGS

There is no clock in baseball. You have to get 27 outs, and then you can go home. That's why you never leave a game early. You just don't know what's going to happen next.

But sometimes 27 outs aren't enough.

It's free baseball, and it could go all night. Tense. Exhilarating. And conventional wisdom is tossed. Everything is on the table, because all it takes to win is a single run.

That's why here in extras we've got a bit of everything trivia-wise: otherworldly All-Star performances, rookie superstars, clutch veterans, and an extremely costly error ...

Finish strong.

TOP OF THE TENTH

Q181: Jeff Bagwell was a fourth-round draft pick of the Boston Red Sox in the 1989 amateur draft. Who did the Astros trade to the Red Sox in exchange for Bagwell in 1990?
  a) Danny Darwin
  b) Jim Clancy
  c) Bill Gullickson
  d) Larry Anderson

Q182: This rookie pitcher was 14-3 in 28 games (20 starts) for a league best .824 winning percentage. He was the first (and through 2019, the only) rookie pitcher in Astros history to lead the league in a major statistical category. Which player accomplished this feat?
  a) Larry Dierker
  b) Scott Elarton
  c) Roy Oswalt
  d) Mike Hampton

Q183: This pitcher began a season with five consecutive starts in which he gave up two, four, one, three, and three hits. Houston won all five starts—and his record was 4-0, with 48 strikeouts and just 13 hits in 37 2/3 innings of work. Arguably it's the greatest start to a season in franchise history. Who posted these extraordinary numbers?
  a) Nolan Ryan
  b) Gerrit Cole
  c) Mike Scott
  d) J.R. Richard

Q184: Cesar Cedeno hit for the first cycle in Astros history in 1972. The most recent cycle (through 2019) belongs to Brandon Barnes in

2013. Who was the first (and, so far, only) player in franchise history to hit for two cycles?
   a) Cesar Cedeno
   b) Bob Watson
   c) Andujar Cedeno
   d) Luke Scott

Q185: One player hit for the cycle with the Astros—but later switched teams, and leagues, and hit for a second cycle. Who was the first player in MLB history to hit for the cycle in both the AL and NL?
   a) Cesar Cedeno
   b) Bob Watson
   c) Andujar Cedeno
   d) Luke Scott

Q186: Only one pitcher (through 2019) has thrown *two* no-hitters for the Astros. Who achieved this remarkable feat?
   a) Nolan Ryan
   b) Mike Scott
   c) Larry Dierker
   d) Don Wilson

Q187: Yordan Alvarez hit a home run during his MLB debut on June 9, 2019. He was just the seventh rookie in franchise history to achieve that feat. Who was the first?
   a) Ken Caminiti
   b) Craig Biggio
   c) Glenn Davis
   d) George Springer

Q188: This pitcher was the first in MLB history to pitch a complete game no-hitter … and lose. He lost 1-0 to the Cincinnati Reds on April 23, 1964—despite giving up no hits and just two walks. Cincinnati scored the game's only run in the ninth thanks to a two-base throwing error—*by the pitcher!*—on a ball hit back to the mound, and a two-out fielding error by the second baseman. Who pitched a gem but lost this game?

a) Ken Johnson
b) Bob Bruce
c) Turk Farrell
d) Don Nottebart

Q189: Jeff Bagwell was the first player in Astros history to hit an Opening Day home run in three consecutive seasons (1994-96). Who tied this franchise record with an Opening Day home run in 2019?

a) Carlos Correa
b) Jose Altuve
c) Alex Bregman
d) George Springer

Q190: This player hit 10 "late and close" home runs in a single-season. Clutch is great. Clutch with power? That's special. Who holds this franchise record?

a) Lance Berkman
b) Jeff Bagwell
c) Jim Wynn
d) Carlos Lee

TOP OF THE TENTH ANSWER KEY

181: d. Larry Anderson.

182: c. Roy Oswalt (2001).

183: d. J.R. Richard (1980).

184: a. Cesar Cedeno (August 1972, August 1976).

185: b. Bob Watson (June 1977, Astros; September 1979, Red Sox).

186: d. Don Wilson (June 1967, May 1969).

187: a. Ken Caminiti (July 1987).

188: a. Ken Johnson.

189: d. George Springer.

190: a. Lance Berkman (2008).

BOTTOM OF THE TENTH

Q191: This player hit 55 "late and close" home runs in his career. Who holds this franchise record?
   a) Glenn Davis
   b) Jeff Bagwell
   c) Lance Berkman
   d) Craig Biggio

Q192: This player had 215 "late and close" RBIs in his career. Who holds this franchise record?
   a) Glenn Davis
   b) Jeff Bagwell
   c) Lance Berkman
   d) Craig Biggio

Q193: These teammates hit back-to-back home runs in the All-Star Game—a feat that had happened only once previously in MLB history. Which duo achieved this feat?
   a) Ken Caminiti/Craig Biggio
   b) Alex Bregman/George Springer
   c) Lance Berkman/Moises Alou
   d) Miguel Tejada/Hunter Pence

Q194: And a follow-up … which former Astros player was one of the teammates that hit back-to-back All-Star home runs for the first time in MLB history?
   a) Joe Morgan
   b) Jim Wynn
   c) Rusty Staub
   d) Bob Watson

Q195: In 1963, Ken Johnson made three consecutive starts in which he pitched at least seven innings but did not allow any walks. It's a streak that's been equaled a few times in Astros history but never surpassed. Mike Scott actually had two such streaks—in 1986, and again in 1987. Through 2019, who is the most recent pitcher to build such a streak for the Astros?
   a) Collin McHugh
   b) Roy Oswalt
   c) Lance McCullers
   d) Justin Verlander

Q196: Incredibly, Gerrit Cole had five games in just two seasons from 2018-19 in which he pitched seven-plus scoreless innings and struck out 10 or more batters. The franchise record for a career is 12 such games. Who holds this mark?
   a) Roy Oswalt
   b) Mike Scott
   c) J.R. Richard
   d) Nolan Ryan

Q197: And a follow-up ... J.R. Richard was the first pitcher in Astros history to pitch seven-plus scoreless innings with 10 or more strikeouts in *consecutive* starts. Through 2019, it's been done just one other time by an Astros pitcher. Who else did this for the Astros?
   a) Gerrit Cole
   b) Justin Verlander
   c) Roger Clemens
   d) Roy Oswalt

Q198: The Astrodome was a difficult place to hit home runs. Just imagine—Jeff Bagwell hit 449 career home runs, but only 126 came at home during nine seasons at the Astrodome. He's the only player

in franchise history to hit 20 home runs in a single-season at the Astrodome—a feat he achieved three times. In just five full seasons at Minute Maid Park, Bagwell had three seasons with 20-plus home runs at home … including a franchise record number in the Astros' inaugural 2000 season in their new home ballpark (then known as Enron Field). What is the record number of home runs Bagwell hit at home that season?
   a) 25
   b) 26
   c) 27
   d) 28

Q199: In 2014, Mets pitcher Jacob deGrom tied a major-league record when he began a game by striking out eight consecutive Miami Marlins. Who was the first pitcher in major-league history to achieve this feat in a start for the Astros against the Los Angeles Dodgers?
   a) Mike Scott
   b) Jim Deshaies
   c) Roy Oswalt
   d) Brandon Backe

Q200: This contemporary star debuted in April, and in May he won Rookie of the Month honors. It helped that he was the first rookie since Rudy York in 1937 to hit seven home runs in a span of seven games. Whose career began in such historic fashion?
   a) Jose Altuve
   b) Carlos Correa
   c) George Springer
   d) Alex Bregman

BOTTOM OF THE TENTH ANSWER KEY

191: b. Jeff Bagwell.

192: d. Craig Biggio.

193: b. Alex Bregman/George Springer.

194: b. Jim Wynn (1975, Dodgers, w/Steve Garvey).

195: a. Collin McHugh (2014).

196: d. Nolan Ryan.

197: c. Roger Clemens (2004).

198: d. 28.

199: b. Jim Deshaies (1986).

200: c. George Springer (2014).

ABOUT THE AUTHOR

Tucker Elliot is a former teacher, coach, and athletic director. He has visited schools on four continents and more than twenty countries as a volunteer or an invited speaker/lecturer. He lives in Florida and Korea.

e-Books by Tucker Elliot

The Day Before 9/11

The Memory of Hope

The Rainy Season

Third Ring Children

The Other Side of the River

Baseball Books by Tucker Elliot

Los Angeles Dodgers IQ: The Ultimate Test of True Fandom

Baltimore Orioles IQ: The Ultimate Test of True Fandom

Cincinnati Reds IQ: The Ultimate Test of True Fandom

Major League Baseball IQ: The Ultimate Test of True Fandom

Tampa Bay Rays IQ: The Ultimate Test of True Fandom

Atlanta Braves IQ: The Ultimate Test of True Fandom

Cleveland Indians IQ: The Ultimate Test of True Fandom

New York Yankees IQ: The Ultimate Test of True Fandom

San Francisco Giants IQ: The Ultimate Test of True Fandom

Washington Nationals IQ: The Ultimate Test of True Fandom

Atlanta Braves: An Interactive Guide to the World of Sports

Boston Red Sox: An Interactive Guide to the World of Sports

San Francisco Giants: An Interactive Guide to the World of Sports

51 Questions for the Diehard Fan: New York Yankees

51 Questions for the Diehard Fan: Atlanta Braves

51 Questions for the Diehard Fan: Baltimore Orioles

BLACK MESA

Visit us on the web to learn more:

www.blackmesabooks.com

SOURCES

Baseball-Reference.com (Play Index)

FanGraphs.com

MLB.com (and the official team sites through MLB.com)

BaseballHallofFame.org

ESPN.com

SABR.org

Baseball-Almanac.com

Elias Sports Bureau

www.ingramcontent.com/pod-product-compliance
Lightning Source LLC
Chambersburg PA
CBHW061444040426
42450CB00007B/1208